LINCOLN PUBLIC LIBRARY

3 4864 00020 7190

THESE ROOMS

D1484531

SUZANNE E. BERGER
THESE ROOMS

PENMAEN PRESS 1979

For
my mother and for my father
and for Michael

Acknowledgment is made to the following publications
for poems or versions of poems which appeared
in them, under the name of Suzanne Berger Rioff:

Antaeus: "Two"; *Arion's Dolphin*: "Madrigal"; *Artists' in Residence Magazine*: "Prayer at 2:45 in the Morning" (formerly, "Passage"); *Aspen Leaves*: "Desert," "My Grandmother's Braids"; *Boston University Magazine*: "The Only Time"; *Cimarron Review*: "Romance for Chagall"; *Dr. Generosity's Almanac*: "Affliction: *Blattaria,* the Common Roach," "Greetings"; *The New Yorker*: "Trout"; *No More Masks* (Doubleday anthology): "Seduction"; *Perspective*: "New Pig-Keeper" (formerly, "Viewing the Sow"); *The Phoenix*: "Choice"; *Ploughshares*: "Your Life: An Invention," "For the Father"; *The Real Paper*: "The Mending," "Box," "Dolphins,"
"In the Garden"; *Women Poems II*: "The Voyeur"

From TO THE LIGHTHOUSE by Virginia Woolf, copyright 1927,
by Harcourt Brace Jovanovitch, Inc.; renewed, 1955, by
Leonard Woolf. Reprinted by permission of the publisher.

Jan 1980

Copyright 1979 by Suzanne E. Berger
Wood engraving copyright 1979 by Mindell Dubansky
All rights reserved

First Edition
Library of Congress Catalogue Number 79-83711
Hardcover edition ISBN 0-915778-29-7
Paperback edition ISBN 0-915778-28-9

Publication of this book was made possible by grants from the
National Endowment for the Arts (Washington, D.C.) and
the Massachusetts Council on the Arts & Humanities.

821
BERGER,S.E.

CONTENTS

So with the house empty and the doors locked and the mattresses rolled round, those stray airs, advance guards of great armies, blustered in, brushed bare boards, nibbled and fanned, met nothing in the bedroom or drawing-room that wholly resisted them but only hangings that flapped, wood that creaked, the bare legs of tables, saucepans and china already furred, tarnished, cracked. What people had shed and left — a pair of shoes, a shooting cap, some faded skirts and coats in wardrobes — those alone kept the human shape and in the emptiness indicated how once they were filled and animated; how once hands were busy with hooks and buttons; how once the looking-glass had held a face; had held a world hollowed out in which a figure turned, a hand flashed, a door opened, in came children rushing and tumbling; and went out again. Now, day after day, light turned, like a flower reflected in water, its clear image on the wall opposite. Only the shadows of trees, flourishing in the wind, made obeisance on the wall, and for a moment darkened the pool in which light reflected itself; or birds, flying, made a soft spot flutter slowly across the bedroom floor.

Virginia Woolf, *To the Lighthouse*

Part One

THE MENDING

Where I am gray
ignite me and shine me
over the waves
like long birds gleaming

Where I am cold or heavy
lift my arms high
to the hot clouds
who bless us
let me learn from their sweat
how to move, how to labor

When I am voiceless
be my lips
when I go off like a shudder
bring me back some blue boots
to climb so again
to my self

Where I have no life
weave me a ribbon
to tie around
the boisterous gifts
that laugh in the night

When I have no song
and am utterly empty
move and rub me
to a ripe cello note
a warbling deeper
than the moon

And when I am blind
with the vast haze
around me
come to me, mend me
sweep over me
like white spring wind

Then graze
in my radiant meadow
where even the stars
could feast

DESERT

For a long time
I stand, listening
to the fog's hushed mouth
against the bedroom window.
The belly I touch is quiet
as a desert,
as smooth and as flowerless.

There is the moon, of course,
that mindless accomplice
whose dull sheen
gets through my veins
like a serum.
Tonight I remember everything,
tonight I am touching
at memory
like a dangerous harp:

how the dirt of my flesh
went unrooted, then,
as my legs were fixed
in an odd ballet.
How the anesthetic grabbed
like a shaman
who gave me the dream
of my grandfather standing over me
dressed in endless green . . .

He never knew how I lay there,
thinking myself a jewel
to be picked over and shined:
I did not pour rubies.

It was only the blood
of a thin weed ungrowing,
then dead,
the opaque eyes gone blind.
Tonight I wonder
if there was a choke,
or an angry thumb at me.
And what sound did
the broken sleep make, breaking?

Here there is no noise:
only the shrill thought
of a beginning of a forehead
that melted,
the beginning of a hand
that uncoiled.
How the new ear went finally deaf,
by a smack of salt, or suck of air,
I do not know. . .

Only at some moments, alone,
I remember imagining
a small mouthful of Kyrie there
singing on in the dark.
And I try to trace
it was nothing, nothing,
on the mute-faced glass.

YOUR LIFE: AN INVENTION

You walk into the orchard:
peaches flop in a globe of shifting green
Here is the sister who left you,
her hair a rowdy auburn
against that fluid summer

You are the hustlers of peaches

You ring the peaches down, down like churchbells
In the faraway Idaho town,
the parishioners do not hear you
You splurge home with an acre of fruit
Bougainvillaea quakes when you get there

The door is a mirror which blows open

Home, in the mother's blue nightgown,
in the father's gabardine sleeves
There is the invalid sleep of old resorts:
your own sleep enters like thick black wine
You dream of peaches and the birthmarks on peaches

You are awakened by your sister

Both of you are dressed in ice,
like root-lace exposed in winter
You are framed in a tall brick fireplace
where your childhood sits, like a cooking stone
She feeds it small creatures of wood

You, vigilant, watch everything melt

Everything goes away, away:
the house is a bruise, the shutters splinter
The sparse ash of gabardine pricks the air
The mirror reflects back
a blaze of exits

The peach-pickers drop their bags

There was never an orchard, she says
We never lived in Idaho
Again, you walk into the orchard
Don't you see there were peaches! you whisper
The orchard had wings to take us away!

The peaches ring as you stand there,
knee-deep in the salvage, your beautiful lies

TROUT

A black blush surfaces,
the trout nibbling the moon
on the water.

Gift-wrapped in a silver daze,
a slow swim, it glides
to the pond edge where I wait:
is this a flirt,
a suicide?
Lidless eyes trance inward,

keeping some close count.
The others move to center,
a dark cluster there:
is it an invalid
who needs a rubdown?
Ecclesiastes begging an ear?
The only crazed one on the ward?
The trout nods and sways,

fins against my salty hands.
Passively, its belly rubs,
then shadows like a lover.
I can feel
the bulged heart pump,
a small red fever.

And then the trout curves off,
a soft bag of hieroglyphs,
secret-monger.

MY GRANDMOTHER'S BRAIDS

Lady of tunnel-gray eyes,
second to touch me when I was born,
three days I watched you,
bound to bed and rubber tubes,
die slowly there
in the burnt-out yellow of hospital light.
Even I, for hours, was quiet.

What little I knew:
That you walked behind your sister,
San Francisco's dazzler,
less glittery than she was,
at forty still her servant, house pet.
You pulled in her gorgeous laundry,
while she pulled in the pearls.

That you dragged a bag
of dark things with you,
a bourbon-drinking lady
who each night flicked off the lamps and sat.
Near midnight, Mother would find you, rocking:
There were invisible spiders
askew in your Irish pulse.

Yesterday, hospital days,
I found you lying there
with sheets flung off like old scarves,
your legs open wide to the universe,
for once, in your oblivion.
I saw the frailest tuft of grandmother-hair,
proof of aged woman-sorrow.

Thin as a baby crane's, your legs,
on which a swarm of veins went wild,
your ankles wretched with elastic.
I came with the faded braids I found,
boxed away since you were twenty.
Dusty black, they held that time like satin chains:
    I held them like an heirloom.

    Before you fell asleep that day
      you asked,
    Who'd want those awful things?

BOX
(for Joan)

This box does not reside in a dream:
if it had eyes, it would be the moist eyes
the childless imagine for a child.
If color, the greenish dandelion stems
the dead would bring back in their hair, visiting.
If motion, the pure rocking of a pulse
that finds, like a red crystal,
another pulse in the dark.

I know it is there, I cannot see it:
perhaps it is behind me,
or living on the telephone wires
that move in the agitated wind.
But with his one hand,
an amputee could open the same lid that broke
his other one before,
and watch the infinite mirrors of the box
give back the image of his lost fingers,
shining.

TWO

Their own trash excites them, they sneak around
        in broad daylight digging for protein.
She looks like a refugee, he is very fat.
Periodically, she throws herself out the window,
periodically, he eats her heart away like a cancer.
They do not speak, they do not.
Across from each other every night, they wave,
        they bite, they stooge each other out.
Their union is strange, she wishes him dead.
Their union is strange, he wants her to dance
        on steeples like a witch in pain.
Across their wide rooms, they screech and parrot.
The sun goes ash when they look at it,
odd odors develop when they touch or sit near.
They have expensive tastes, they like only
        the richest fillets of each other.
They have ceremonies in which they take rubber knives
        and draw real blood.
When they make love, it is the sound of dry cloth rustling.
Their love is the great wing of a young bat
        that covers them in the dusk.
They are very strange, their own trash excites them.

NEW PIG-KEEPER

As the sow slept on,
there was nothing pinker,
more absolute:
the woman heard the blunt snout
so humanly blow and retort.

The fanfare, the pandemonium!
The sound was the deep roar
of a dreamless pig,
a throne of flesh.
The sow drooled, rolling over,
flashing a nagtooth big as a horn.

Like decadent sheets,
manure spread around her,
sleeping in her odd boudoir.
Flapped and hairy, the old sow-ears
heard echoes and echoes of hay.
A deafness rang in the woman's ears.

When the sow coughed,
the barn coughed back,
and a rat slid over her pig-perfect haunches.
She woke up blinking tiny eyes,
vague and uneven as scars.

Her whole body a grunting stomach,
a bloat of sighs!
Wooden-toed, the balding queen of fat
stood up, a miracle.
The woman thought of kingdoms, exiles.

Obtrusively, the sow teats showed;
little fingers,
they touched and nibbled the floor.
And then she opened her freckled mouth
to show a universe of buds and warts,
slop-tasters each and all.

Each tooth was yellow,
a raggedy soldier.
And a colossal tongue,
hungry as a long shovel,
curious and dreamy.
The woman thought of appetites.

Open-mouthed, the pig stood there,
where the woman imagined falling in,
deftly as a fly.
The woman stared, locked in:
New pig-keeper.

AFFLICTION: BLATTARIA, *THE COMMON ROACH*

Open the door.
Out they swell, a mahogany flood, out
of the cream, the door-hinge, the plaster.
                    The little pets

            are coming sly.
Inside their husks, black pharaohs and czars!
They multiply like a smear of night.
                    Forky legs

            pinch walls, crawl
close, their dream a dream of bread and oil and us:
                    For we are captives,

            we are the sweetmeat.
Feel their hungers twitch, they are watching
greasy-eyed, roaming over our rooms.
                    Watch them watch

            disperse, pointillize.
From the ceiling, they may drop one by one
down to the breeding scalp or belly
                    to brew there

            then scurry.
            Right there.
            Here.

MADRIGAL

Driving home by the Charles
each night at five-fifteen
I hate my life

its bored windows
its bone-gray compromise

its distant way
of cracking me
into a splinter-woman
dangerously invisible

I'd wish to be green
and wet as a virgin

a green bottomless as fish
or the infant nipples of lilacs

to burst out of myself
dive far into space
all blue all helium all quartz
dreaming against
some god-high eave

my hair would float
in a glitter of heat
I would suck the buds
of young cherry trees
setting them on fire with me

while I madden the river
with my wonderful hands

I want to be the crushed and lovely moment
between the bloom of bellies

everything would touch me
fingers ankles shoulders sweat
everywhere I would live

touch for touch
I'd be a crystal
forming white-hot
between lovers going down

the tiny me-cry belly
in between the two

IN THE GARDEN
(for Michael)

The night she died, you watched
the transparent garden spiders
cross over to midnight, now one, now two,
on their dusty August tightropes;
her half-acre emptied out for you,
bleached earth where she had tramped,
in her bandanna, with spade and trowel.

Now, sowing and reaping, weeding and pulling,
you restore the garden.
In the underground radiance,
seeds breathe, onions begin to bubble.
Early mornings, you coach the marigolds
and wait for the tight rose-hammers
to release bright noise of red and yellow.

In gloves caked with soil,
how you poke and mend there,
stalker of beetles and aphids,
guardian angel of zucchini.
By your sweat, new roots splurge,
grief-takers in the humid dirt.
Then, subdued and drinking whiskey,
you bask in the ordinary leaf-shine:
green voltage to burn away the dark.

Part Two

MORNINGS

Quiet until now,
that moment like a startled bird
darts between us at our meal:
It was in the morning,
you stood at the counter,
looking at the snow.
Father came up behind you,
and cupped your breasts,
and held them for a long time.
I stood in the doorway, watching.

That Saturday morning was newborn
in the mother-and-father light:
your breasts like pears
that never really shaped
until I watched him shine them.
Look how we always shelve our breasts,
indelicately, on top of tables.

Yesterday, in the long mirror,
I surveyed the thickened waist
I haven't earned, as you did.
Hands on hips, alert to rustlings
on my small estate,
I heard nothing but silence.
I saw only ribbons leftover from Christmas,
the cat flung like a shawl on the blanket,
an old tulip of dark blood
on my twice-washed sheets:
I said aloud to my rooms,
In my house will it always be this quiet?

Years from now, perhaps,
I will come to this same table,
and ask an unborn daughter:
Tell me about the time
you saw him cup my breasts with tender hands,
and how you stayed for a long time,
that morning,
standing in the doorway, watching.

INSTRUCTIONS TO THE PATIENT

You must remember the vagary
of your conception
the stun of birth's lips
the sly quiet hands
who bathed you in salt   in honey
rebuked until you wailed with love

How rain and grease smelled
hiding in your mother's hair
and your father's shoes
drying up like pods near the oven

You must remember words   words
the weight of them
like archangels   like iron gloves
How first they were shy animals
and then they were javelins
coming too swiftly back toward you

You must remember fire's first bruise
persistent as a birthmark
and all the rooms you entered
with fingers crossed against the night

You must remember the fevers
singeing you too ragged for sleep
And what made you huddle under the quilt
what made you cringe under the hedge

You must remember the first night
of a god blooming out in your mouth
the hushed first night you first made love
and made your own prehistory
the legs spread out like a random giving of roses
the first night the roses broke their necks

You must remember friends
how their smiles hooked to yours in a tryst
then later their voices shaking with your lies
Then some of their voices torn apart

What tricks you performed
with a dazzling grace
How you took the longest fall
through a netless smother of air
where you landed
what you lost   what fell off

You must remember the summer-white fields
the queen anne's lace   the wire
the strange thud of voices in barred rooms
where they waged war   like an engine

You must remember the smell of sickness
the shape of your grandfather's brass knuckle hand
as he tried to beat death away   away
It came back like a glutton   a wolf

You must remember the menace
that ate in your heart
as a pilgrim eats journeys

How all the miles
of coming and going crossed over your life
like twisted sutures   or trenches

And of all this

You must remember
all the uncertain charities
all the unending soft fists in the dark

VITA

Airtight, the photograph
flickers like a lost moth
on the ragged wall:
I mewl behind the shadowy glass,
lips open for first words
winging in like starlings,
family wisdom, Gerber's peas.
Smiling is my mother's country,
perfect as my baby fists.

Her bathrobe is scattered
with flannel wildflowers,
her breasts rang out then
with my rapid-angle sucking.

Crew-cut, blonder than the Dog Star,
my father surveys me,
a pink icon, untouchable.

Love crackled like sheets of foil,
while cherry pipe-smoke filled the air.

I remember how she beat
the Texas rattlesnakes away
with golf-clubs,
how he "measured" for Standard Oil.
I dreamed him in an aqualung, rubber mask,
swimming through a dark tank,
drowning in a smother of grease.
They pulled me from the sky one night,
they said, just like a dazzling comet.

Two thousand miles from Texas now,
their house constricts with summer heat,
loss moves through the rooms
like a long double hook.

In one picture, her eyes grow certain
we all are trapped in an accident
that makes us invisible.

She, slowly watching the world
as one with shears
watches over a poisonous garden.

In another, my father still wears
his dusty Air Force cap
like a jutting prow.
Ears grown deaf from the B-17 pandemonium,
and the freezing noise
around him now,
he tiptoes near a precipice—
I tiptoe in their broken kingdom:
Crybaby, exile, daughter.

A COLD DOZE

Officer, I am lying on the pavement
of this underground garage
because I heard the sound
of someone sobbing, between wet tires.

I am going only twenty on the slick Southeast expressway
because speed needs a stout heart, and I have none.
I am more weather than driver,
becoming ribs of quick rain, ribs of cold:
the magic asphalt spins the wheels.

Officer, I am looking in the stranger's house,
watching the children eat spaghetti,
watching the lamp above their heads
cover them with a golden fur.
I will not steal anything
but the steam of their talking, their family heat.

I am standing under the street light
to assemble myself for winter, as best I can.
Inside, loneliness breaks the air,
like the sound of many geese, hoarse and forgotten.
Icicles take root, winter wasps are nesting.

Officer, I cannot cry.
This season is a cold doze,
swelling the eyelids, sealing the cells,
lulling the nerves to sleep.

VISITING YOU
    (for T. S.)

The dreamless weather
sleeps like a glacier

In the ice sculpture of you,
something still breathes,
transparent as the embryo
of a bird

Ice in the prickled fur
of a frozen rat,
eyes painted black,
a winter icon

In the nightmare of you,
red pintos graze
in a burning field
of ice shards

Ice, from a tree scar
where once gold sap inched out

Any moment to find you,
I could step into ice,
pull on a crystal skin
I could open the hospital door

But you would be a doll
of blue ice staring out
at someone weeping
like a pilgrim in front of the waters

WOMAN AND HORSE IN FIELD

The thin gray horse
lies down in the meadow
where he will die,
ignored by thistles
and milkweed—
how they blow themselves off,
such silks and blacks,
as the hair of the insane blows.

Someone walks there,
a woman trembling through the field
like a searcher
for lost relatives:
the grass clatters
in the warm wind.

Above, a hawk arcs,
a cut-out shape torn
from a papery sky,
blooming out like a cry
in the night.

The hunger in the meadow.
The quiet ribs,
the silent beak of the hawk,
the brittle sway of weeds:
All move her on,
a lens of nightmare
near her eyes.

And when the moon
rings whitely down,
she lies down near the horse,
makes an armband of thistles,
and sings
of all the brutal opulence.

THE SEDUCTION

Open me like a meadow lily
examine me like an eel
for my mystery
my electric blue swim

Put me together
I am many chinks of broken light
Gently prod me to my country
where the mileage is green and wide
Gather my hills
to their plumpness
Name my rivers
Count the seconds
it takes to pry me open
to make me pour

Love, love me
Turn my thistle-cloth to satin
where we lie
like rosy Egyptian scarabs
Love me
for I am often singular
Alone, I break and steal
and run, delinquent
Make me your moon-mate
your daughter
your prism
Mend my surfaces
be my mirror
my great hush

Be the light
by which my angles, my crevices
are explored
Miner, mine me
I am dark and rich
The caves are hung
with my secrets, my hair
Make me peaceful
make me chirp
Hide me
in the warm giant boot
of your human grace
Blush me
pull me out of pallor

Imagine me
in the white furry breath
of your dreaming
Make me still
Make me naked
Make me an animal
who loves its own tongue

GREETINGS

old mr. elrod reels down the street
(a saint with a baby carriage
bursting with ten-cent junk
and holiness)

tilda (loving him every night
while the ceiling falls down like clouds
and chickens crackle in the washing machine)
calls

and mr. elrod lifting his hat
(unloading two madonnas, three corsets
a bicycle wheel) salutes her
most bountifully

FOR THE FATHER
(later acquitted of the drowning)

There was the pond,
trout-filled, dark green.
Child-shaped for the father
since the child was born.
But deeper.

There was the sour brown meadow,
the blue jays moving
against his ears.
The father walked through,
lonelier than anyone.

There was the huge doll-son
he carried, breathing heavy
in his arms.
On the child's cheek was spittle,
like a trickle of speech.

There was the body the father called
My aging cabbage. Cabbage.
Gently, he pushed the body under water.
There were the half-moon eyelids
opening up like milky lilies,
then closing while the father's heart
pumped out of his widening mouth.

DOLPHINS
(after reading Anne Sexton's 45 *Mercy Street*)

Bathed all day in silver oil,
they surface, pink noses dividing
the momentary air.
Arched, they leap up — a flash of spines —
spring back to the humid sea,
quick-curving like so many plump commas.

Such colossal skin,
as if pulled on like gleaming stockings
just before this diamond ballet.
Warbling stacatto like flutes,
chuckling deep like babies,
the dolphins have tender eyes.

And so, your stanzas ride and dive
to break the margins of your death.
Fins up and radar shining,
your poems glint on —
a stretch of extended silver
lively in a grieving sea.

POSSESSED
(at Pilgrim Heights, Cape Cod)

There goes the ocean
as it perishes and brims
like a blue orchard of desiring women

There go the beach shacks
the thin yellow roofs
withdrawing into winter night

There go the shadows of pilgrims
flaring their axes and bones underground

Then suddenly

There go the feet of your usual body
your hands, your stiffly-seeing eye

And the ocean moves into you
naming the forgotten parts
lifting the old cells off you

And you remember nothing
language leaves you like a numb relative

The ocean pours over you, into you
begging you to be its skin
to climb into its nerves and muscle

To make you hers, all hers
until nearly bodiless
you drift away with her

You arch with her
and nothing knows you
but the gallop you ride together

You ring, you deepen
you rock open as a milkweed

And then
there goes your other life

Part Three

CHOICE

Black, fierce as Cain
then momentary
as ellipsis
or miracle

The river and I
breathing together
Clear black laceration of water
Lip to lip

Drugged on her offering
My arm caught on a slippery branch
holding me back
from her garden
of freezing oblivion

The cutting rocks poke out
from the tug of yellow current
Fish near the mouth like silver tongues
This river, the church of many windows
a pure house without echoes

Silk cleavers of water
dividing me
into the humming color of water
I, the endless downstream
twin of river flowing
into garden

But the bank where my father
is walking
But the distant bank where
my brother calls
On the bank there is another breathing

And I do not want drowning
nor the garden
where memory splays
on cold granite flowers
Where, piecemeal, the fingers find the mud

Suddenly, I feel my arm
is a long stone growing
a bridge hardening
is the will stretched and stuck

Half in water, half in daze
the river-smell of slaughter
bends me back
and I lie on the mulchy bank

and breathe like a just-slapped baby

THE VOYEUR

Today I must watch myself as
I would watch a breathing film:

As if drowning into eight o'clock,
she pulls herself from wooden sheets.

The weather is brittle gold,
the wind is a fist at the door.

Softly she brushes lank hair.
The bathroom steam is angelic at her breasts.

A green blouse drags from the closet.
There are rituals of coffee, of waiting for.

Downstairs, the after-summer flies
bend off the screen in dark parabolas.

She sweeps at them,
until there is a mound of black.

The veined wings glow.
Perhaps there is the courage, only,
for watching small things die.

On the writing pad, the words:
"Perhaps the foetus floats off Long Island
in the bilge of factories."

The cat shadows her, eyes the color of burnt agates.
Claws scraping the floor
like prayer beads, singly dropped.

Her hands flutter, as if adjusting the air.
She watches the reel unwind.

THE LETTING GO

I

At last, I have found it,
it moves on
like a knife still wet
from the cut fruit

II

Fourteen years ago,
in the peach orchard
black insects gnawing the new crop

I imagined the smoke of their hot teeth
grinding at the wood

There is smoke still left on me,
the scar still alive
from your heated vowels
against my cheek

III

Smoke, sleeping beside me like a twin

Under the breasts a half-moon of smoke

Smoke under the eyelids
like an endless movie

Smoke in thick layers over butter,
in the fat veins of meat

Smoke fogging the mirrors in the belly
where there should be the clearest lens

Smoke between the legs like a requiem

Smoke lying down in a house
where even the walls have been stolen

Smoke, the dust of a name,
letters crying back for their owner

Smoke, the tongue winding itself
backwards on a spool of black

IV

In Africa, a tribe plants a pig-corpse
in the spring — jubilation, jubilation

Underground, the maggots fattening like pearls,
luminous and sweet

In fall, they dig up the corpse
and give the plumpest worm
to the most beautiful woman

After the pink feast of its flesh,
she spreads her palm-oiled limbs,
her face flowing down like a black river
for the gift and her own abundance

Pearl of you, pearl flinging me back to Ohio
where it is always April
in the rotting mile of peaches

V

Smoke, you rise before me like a slave ship

Smoke, the mad are whimpering for their breakfasts

Smoke, where am I?
Why does this room have brown paper bags
collapsing in corners?

Where is the name burned off like a birthmark?

VI

What do I do with it, this imperfect night?
It is filled with the energy of sirens
with despair balanced like a tripod

This night tearing a hole in the sky
ragged as kelp or a wound

In this night, my body is two enemies
that meet wearing each other's faces

Smoke, my arms bend down like plump bags of old peaches

VII

Night and smoke, smoke and night —
milk turned to brine, eyes to flat mica, roads closed

Dust moving in corners like a nervous claw

Jubilation, your blood and mine
drifting across the calendar
like a thick sap of rubies

The new skin reaching through the old smoke,
reaching over the scar
in a long dream of red amber,
in the letting go

Jubilation, it will be finished

Jubilation, it will not awake

PRAYER AT 2:45 IN THE MORNING
(for Polly)

although these years
trespass
ceremoniously

there are
the small repairs

in the snag of flesh
at midnight
and a decent hosanna
at dawn

THE ONLY TIME

This is the only time,
the only pulse that saves us.
Your body strays me from dirges, from quiet,
and I cry like an angel-hawk when it happens.
Love, let there be no air, no words between us
as I labor over you like a poem of nerves,
and the silky play goes on and on,
a play of fragrance, of opulence.
You pouring pure as three white storms,
me singing back like an earth
crying for health, an earth who knows
                              for a moment
no lies, no famine, no years.
With this, we ride away the fevers,
we ride each other off to a country far
                              and secret-keeping.
With this, we are also like feasting planets
who breathe in each other's mouths.
Our toiling is huge, our sweat like yeast,
and we name ourselves lavish, we name ourselves *Yes.*
This is the plate where we eat,
and I only eat to live.

BETRAYAL

The tongue
of all voices
cannot speak,
stuck to its vowels,
lies,
grim accusations
       of owners.

In speechless mahogany,
clocks drone and sleep
in this room of walls:
how we chew
on the unintelligible
like cow fodder,
spitting it out
       in words.

How, sadly,
self to another,
the mouth blows
like a plastic horn.
Words mutating
as they come out,
       like sly new flowers.

We make no sense,
our lips cannot form
a we-cry,
we jump off
endless, life-long cliffs
while words fall

from our mouths,
       like so much shale.

A match,
kissing itself away in water,
makes more sense.
Or the black clothes
of nuns
dazzling the air
       like verbs.

ROMANCE, FOR CHAGALL

cows float like brides
    or brides float like cows
    when papa chagall dances around
        his creation
and the samovar brims to a spring

so it is papa chagall and his village
    all blasted with music and myth
    the fiddler picks c-sharps
        from a chorus of flowers
that sings and bows us
        a rubied cantata

the lovers tilt high over wedding steeples
    and a rooster seduces
    the blue night-horse
        while chagall watches
his eyes a prism of whimsy

but often a bird-like phantom
    flies black in the wedding dream
    it may topple the lovers
        back to earth
and the rooster back
        to his earthly pen

INFIDELS

The old writer shrinks in
He regards the blackening roses and chocolates:
signals of extreme affection

The fisted mother of nightmare
pokes under the sheets, the straps and rubber tubes:
there is the silence of warring cells

The visitors come in to spin
on the beautiful blue disc of his imagination:
he lifts one hand to greet them

It falls like a thin bird,
it is a pale stranger
floating down to the blanket

The health of their hair and eyes
cuts new windows in him

They want to spin, to spin:
when he begins to speak
they lurch forward to grab for his radiant words

His mouth grows plain as an egg,
more vulnerable than his body:
only thin syllables pull out on a string

Their disappointment is absolute:
they chat, then bow to rush their watches on
There are handshakes, damp kisses, umbrellas

If he could move, he would lock the door
and make them wear the size of his face,
the darkening marrow of his bones

NAMENLOSEN

Years ago, God moved in me
like a polished cello,
a grasshopper king.
When I heard the word Omniscience,
I thought of an x-ray vision,
shining across the continents.
Each event was a butterfly floating,
God-sighted and then approved.
Praying, there was an inviolate hug
around my head, a golden oil in my dreams.

In the camp, small Jakab heard
a whispering father call
the Dachau chimneys *Namenlosen*.
Nameless: the high brick thieves
chugging up ashes, dazed bones,
punctual as the midnight
each day had come to be.

I try, Jakab, as the blind try
to locate a voice to pull them out
from a deep-watered gray.
In this room, I stand muttering:
Locate faith and fix it
like a gleaming pin to hold up
the fragile, hazardous house.
A joist, a beam, an unbreakable roof.

But Jakab, you rise up again, you move
like a crack in the wall, inch by inch.
Jakab, what was that lung of dark light

who breathed the world those years,
as your fists beat
like the extinct wings of birds
against the oven air?

MEDITATION IN WISCONSIN

A whitened jewel,
the lake shines back
at the house,
vacant twelve years.

Inside, the portraits gaze,
bored as parkbenches for gossip:
the spasms of aunts' crying,
undone with divorce
and smothered with heirlooms.
The grandfather's asthma
nibbling his lovely lungs.
Here, shrill blue-greens
of the garish sunroom
blurred to a dim beige hush.

Secrets cluster there,
in the framed pastels, the oils:
the first wife skating
in white mink muff, Chicago 1902.
The third one staring
from cocaine-bruised eyes
at me, a photo on the other wall:
eight years old,
balanced on an aquaplane,
a part-girl fish in braids.

I ran through the North room,
dazzled with mirrors,
but the red-velvet room finally caught me,
the room of stuffed eagles and owls,

where the Victorian clock
lost an hour each day,
forgetful and forgetting us.
My memory stutters on five o'clock,
it is always five o'clock in the house.
Time for old-fashioneds and camembert.

Down the long halls, the eloquent sounds
acutely shadow, then halt:
drunkenly, a grandmother played Chopin
all through one August,
clutching a lacy midnight to her breast
until it stayed there.
Now the piano is stuck
to its tone-deaf octaves,
the keys asleep like ivory bats
in a closed cave of mahogany.

The shower pipes sang, knowing us,
then gave up to a rusty quiet.
Even the clack of croquet mallets
is now frozen in the snowy yard.
So what noise now moves the smoky dust
to hide like animals in corners?
And lost, the sound of my grandfather
demanding in German guttural
that his pink grapefruit be segmented
precisely as his money.

Now what bodiless rags
slide the child-riding bannisters,
who eats the invisible muffins, the grief?

Who rides on the skeleton swing,
long since twisted off by wind
from the aging boathouse roof?
Dangerously, love swung there,
out over the water,
as the slats pressed hard as steel wings
against my sixteen-year-old back.

Some quiet creature
defiantly nests, sneaking in the place
where furtive touch, bitter jokes and lies,
spilled out like ash all summer,
on green bedspreads and in alcoves.
Here two of us
were conceived and dreaded,
noveau art flashy in an old museum.
This is my hothouse,
my box of small passions.

Blindly, the house withdraws,
an elder whose privacy locks
and does not quaver.
I drop the key in the diminishing, ice-bitten lake.

The house dreams, absolute.

COLOPHON

These Rooms was printed during the summer of 1979 at the Penmaen Press in Lincoln, Massachusetts. Joan Norris and Michael Peich provided editorial assistance. The book was designed and set in Times New Roman by Michael McCurdy. John Kristensen and Penelope Reid printed the edition of 1200 books, from which 200 were hard-bound. These were numbered and signed by the author. Mindell Dubansky cut the wood engraving which appears on the title page.

821   Berger, Suzanne E.

        These rooms.

LINCOLN PUBLIC LIBRARY
LINCOLN, MASS. 01773